W9-CCN-813

Cell Phones and Society

Cell Phones and Teens

Other titles in the *Cell Phones and Society* series include:

Cell Phones
and Teens

Christine Wilcox

San Diego, CA

© 2015 ReferencePoint Press, Inc.
Printed in the United States

For more information, contact:
ReferencePoint Press, Inc.
PO Box 27779
San Diego, CA 92198
www.ReferencePointPress.com

LIBRARY OF CONGRESS CATALOGING-IN-PUBLICATION DATA

Wilcox, Christine.
  Cell phones and teens / by Christine Wilcox.
    pages cm. -- (Cell phones and society)
  Includes bibliographical references and index.
  Audience: Grade 9 to 12.
  ISBN-13: 978-1-60152-666-3 (hardback)
  ISBN-10: 1-60152-666-0 (hardback)
  1. Cell phones and teenagers--Juvenile literature. I. Title.
  HQ799.2.C45W56 2015
  303.48'30835--dc23
                                                2013047988

Contents

A Teen's Most Prized Possession

To sixteen-year-old Philippa Grogan, the idea of living without a cell phone is unthinkable. "I'd rather give up, like, a kidney than my phone," she tells the *Guardian*. "How did you manage before? Carrier pigeons? Letters? Going round each others' houses on *bikes*?"[1] About 78 percent of US teenagers would agree with her, since that is how many carry their own cell phone. Half of those phones are smartphones—powerful computers that put the Internet at their fingertips and give them on-the-go access to social networking sites. They text, they tweet, they "like" each other's photos on Facebook and keep close track of their own "likes." They migrate en masse to new social media apps and drop them so quickly that it is difficult for parents to track their online activity. It is almost impossible for a teenager to have an active social life without a cell phone. In fact, most of their social lives happen on their phones—in the abbreviated text-speak that few adults understand.

> "I'd rather give up, like, a kidney than my phone."[1]
>
> —Philippa Grogan, age sixteen.

Parents worry that the cell phone is changing their children by isolating them from real human socialization, giving them shorter attention spans and less patience, and making them narcissistic. Every technology has an effect on those who use it, but it is not necessarily a bad effect. There is no conclusive evidence that digital technology is any more harmful to teenagers than any other technology, but it has probably given them the most benefits. Cell phones and social networking (it is impossible to talk about one without the other) allow teens to have a level of control in their interactions that no generation has ever had before. They do not have to worry about how they look, how they sound, or whether or not they are blushing or sweating. They can think before they speak, or type, crafting their responses as they craft their identity. According to Amanda Lenhart, a specialist in teens and technology at the Pew Research Center, "Mobile phones and social networking sites make the things teens have always done—defining their own identity, establishing themselves as independent of their parents, looking cool, impressing members of the opposite sex—a whole lot easier."[2]

Dangerous Technology

This is not to say that there are not problems with teen cell phone use. Teens can use their cell phones so compulsively that some experts consider them to be addicted. Compulsive phone use can interfere with sleep, schoolwork, and family relationships. It can also cost teens their lives. Texting while driving kills thousands of teens every year, but even though almost everyone understands the dangers, many teens—and adults—just cannot resist reading an incoming text.

Cell phones and social media are ubiquitous in the lives of today's teenagers. Connecting with friends, defining identities, and establishing independence are all made easier with cell phones.

Spending so much time interacting in virtual spaces also causes what scientists call the online disinhibition effect. Essentially, the more time people spend interacting online, the more they lose the social inhibitions and sense of empathy that keep society running smoothly. A teen is far more likely to toss off a cruel remark in a text or a post than say it in person, and digital spaces can quickly turn vicious. The cell phone is also a favorite tool of bullies, who can launch far more damaging and humiliating attacks with their phones than they can face-to-face.

Teens are also lured into a false sense of security in their digital spaces. Because they have more control, they are often tempted to overshare, forgetting that everything lasts forever on the Internet. They post pictures of themselves drinking or otherwise acting irresponsibly, forgetting that the image may cost them a job or a spot in the college of their choice. Girls sext their boyfriends nude pictures of themselves—because they are in love or want to be—and are shocked when that picture is forwarded to everyone they know. Reputations are ruined for years, and some victims are driven to suicide.

An Indispensable Tool

Still, most experts believe the good outweighs the bad. Cell phones help keep teenagers safe by keeping them connected to their parents, which in turn gives them more autonomy. Smartphones help turn teenagers into technologically savvy adults who have a better chance of becoming leaders and innovators in their fields. One teenager recently created an app that texts the user's location to a loved one right before his or her cell phone battery dies. Another invented a device that can charge a phone battery in less than a minute. And because of cell phone technology, low-income teens around the world have access to the Internet and its educational resources. For all of their risks and benefits, cell phones have become indispensable to adults and teenagers alike.

Cell Phones and Social Development

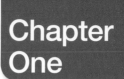

The scene is a familiar one: A group of teenagers are sitting together at the mall. They appear to be friends, yet they are not talking to each other. Instead, each is looking intently at his or her cell phone. Some seem to be texting, while others are simply staring down at their phones' tiny screens, oblivious to what is going on around them. To many adults—especially those who remember talking nonstop with their friends at that age—the teenagers' behavior is bewildering. They wonder why these teens are not interacting with each other.

There is a good chance that at least some of them are. It is not unusual for today's teenagers to carry on private conversations via text message with people who are sitting right next to them. It is also not considered rude to interrupt a face-to-face conversation to respond to a text message or read a social media update. The reason is simple: A modern teen's social life happens on his or her cell phone. When teenagers want to know what is going on in their social circles, they do not ask their friends; they check their phones. And according to a recent survey by the Pew Research Center's Internet & American Life Project, the majority of teenage conversations no longer happen face-to-face. They happen on a cell phone—either in text messages or over social networking sites like Facebook and Twitter.

Growing Up with Digital Technology

Sometimes referred to as *digital natives*, most of today's teenagers grew up with digital technology, and many younger teens do not remember a time when they did not have access to a cell phone. With the introduction of the Motorola RAZR in 2004 (the first cell phone marketed to teens) and then the iPhone in 2007 (the first handheld computer, or smartphone, with a touch screen interface), the cell phone became both an indispensable and highly coveted object to teenagers worldwide. Many teens feel that they must have their

9

phones with them at all times. As one teenager described it, "Leaving home without my phone almost feels like leaving the house naked."[3]

Unlike in years past, when teenagers developed social skills by spending their free time in the same physical space, many of today's teens interact primarily in digital space. "A large part of this generation's social and emotional development is occurring while on the Internet and on cell phones,"[4] explain the authors of a recent report about social media and adolescents. Though teenagers talk about the same things they have always talked about—their peers, their love interests, their parents, the future—their conversations outside of school are no longer limited to phone calls on a landline telephone and the occasional get-together on the weekend. Conversations can now occur at any time—and on the teenager's terms. Texting allows teens to have multiple private conversations, chat in groups, or broadcast their thoughts to whoever wants to listen. Social networking sites allow them to share their lives by posting pictures and commentary throughout the day. As researcher Alice Marwick notes, "Teens send a constant stream of updates to their nearest and dearest, weaving an intimate web between themselves and their friends."[5] Because of this, for a teenager to have a normal social life, a cell phone is now a necessity.

> "Leaving home without my phone almost feels like leaving the house naked."[3]
>
> —Brenna, seventeen-year-old participant in a panel discussion about teens and cell phones.

A Child's First Cell Phone

Of the 78 percent of teenagers who have cell phones, more than half received their first phone as tweens (children aged eight to twelve). However, with the rise in popularity of the smartphone, which has a touch-screen interface that is easy for younger children to manipulate, some kids are getting their first phones even earlier. Xavier Watch has been playing with his father's smartphone since he was four years old. At five he can browse the web and create his own music playlists, and Victor Watch is thinking about getting him his own iPhone. "If I wait until he's a teenager," he told the *Boston Globe*, "when he finally does get one he may go crazy and act out with it to make up for lost time. . . . This way I can at least control the introduc-

Sitting side by side and texting or just looking at online content is a common scenario, visible at almost any location where teens congregate. Much of a teenager's social life these days takes place over the phone.

tion."[6] Watch is not alone in considering getting his preschooler a smartphone. A 2013 survey found that nearly one out of ten children receive their first cell phone by the time they are five.

Though parents like Watch use a cell phone to introduce their kids to technology, most want their children to have a cell phone for safety reasons. "You hear about all these things happening at school," Jackie, the mother of a seventh grader, told researchers. "If there was ever an emergency, I would know that she had it [her cell phone]."[7] Cell phones allow parents to check on their kids at any time, and children have the security of knowing that Mom and Dad are just a phone call

The Popularity of Facebook

Facebook debuted in 2004 as one of the first social networking sites that requires users to supply their own names. It quickly overtook Myspace as the most popular place for teens to gather and share information about their lives. About 94 percent of teenagers have an account on Facebook. The next most popular site is Twitter, used by 26 percent of teens, followed by Instagram, YouTube, Myspace, and Tumblr. Twitter, a microblogging site, is the fastest-growing social media site, followed by Instagram (picture sharing) and Tumblr (short-form blogging).

A 2013 survey by the Pew Research Center found that teens were tiring of the constant drama on Facebook among their friends and were visiting the site less and less frequently. "I think Facebook can be fun, but also it's drama central," one teen girl explained. The drop in teen visits was confirmed later that same year by David Ebersman, Facebook's chief financial officer. Facebook has become a popular networking site with adults, which is another reason that teens are staying away. Still, almost all value their connections on the site enough to keep their accounts active.

Quoted in Amanda Hess, "Teenagers Hate Facebook but They're Not Logging Off," *XX Factor* (blog), *Slate*, May 22, 2013. www.slate.com.

away. Parents also rely on cell phones for what one researcher dubbed microcoordination, which involves working out the logistics of rides, curfew, and so forth. Some even use the cell phone as a parenting tool, monitoring their children's incoming calls and text messages. But very few parents buy a cell phone to encourage their child to be more social. As one mother explained, if her son had a cell phone, he would be "talking too much, for no particular reason, making silly phone calls."[8]

Necessary for a Healthy Social Life

Although kids enjoy the safety and convenience that a cell phone provides, their primary reason for wanting a cell phone is to communicate with friends. The desire to be social is in full force by the time most children reach middle school, which is when a cell phone goes from being coveted status symbol to social necessity. According to a survey by Harris Interactive, a majority of teens say their cell phone is the key to a successful social life. In a separate study, anthropologist Robbie Blinkoff found that teens who tell their parents that they will be excluded or looked down on for not having a cell phone are not just being dramatic. He found that a teen without a cell phone did not have much chance of speaking or socializing with a teen who had one. "If you are not a name or number on my phone book," Blinkoff said, explaining the attitude of the cell phone–carrying teen, "then you are not on my radar screen."[9] In short, being without a cell phone as a teenager can amount to social suicide.

Interestingly, the teenagers in Blinkoff's study did not see anything wrong with this attitude. Neither did fourteen-year-old Casey Schwartz, who told the *Huffington Post* that a girl in her circle of friends was essentially ignored for six months because her iPhone did not have the latest instant messaging software. "She wasn't in the group chat, so we stopped being friends with her," Casey said. "Not because we didn't like her, but we just weren't in contact with her."[10] While this may sound harsh, it represents the reality of teenage life today. Because most of their social lives are either planned or played out on their cell phones, those without phones have no way to participate.

The Popularity of Texting

The most popular communication feature of the cell phone is not the phone itself; it is text messaging. Texting is faster and less interruptive than a phone call or e-mail, and it allows teens to multitask. "It's easier," seventeen-year-old Fadumo Jama explained. "You can have more than one conversation with a lot of people at the same time."[11] Texting also gives teens more control, allowing them to ignore or delay answering messages or avoid uncomfortable face-to-face confrontations. Finally, texting allows teens to have private conversations at any time—even when their parents are nearby. "There are a lot of situations when you don't want to speak out loud," Joseph Konstan, a professor who specializes in human-computer interaction, explains. "[Texting provides] direct access to your friends without it being mediated by parents."[12]

According to the Pew Research Center, texting is now the primary way teens communicate with each other. Sixty-three percent text their friends and family at least once a day—far more often than they use other forms of daily communication (only 39 percent have daily phone conversations with their friends, and only 35 percent physically see each other every day outside of school). Teens exchange an average of 165 texts a day, which does not include conversations in chat applications or on social media platforms like Facebook and Twitter. For seventeen-year-old Andrew, a busy high school student from Nashville, Tennessee, that number is much higher. Andrew plays in a local band, is active in his church, and holds down both a part-time job and an internship. He manages his day with his cell phone, sending text messages to his boss, coworkers, friends, and girlfriend, who is away at college. By noon Andrew has exchanged more than two hundred texts—or a text every ninety seconds—a number many adults find hard to imagine. But as he explained to researchers at Microsoft, phone calls simply take too much time.

Facebook and Other Social Media

While texting is the preferred method for one-on-one conversation, social media sites are teens' preferred gathering spaces. Eight out of ten teens who use the Internet also use some kind of social media—which is commonly defined as any site that allows social interaction. More than half of all teenagers sign on to a social media site at least once a day—many with their cell phones. And while teens use dozens of sites, Facebook is by far the most popular. Of teens who use social media, 94 percent have profiles on Facebook.

Because so many teens are now on Facebook, it has become a kind of social broadcasting center. A survey by the Berkman Center for Internet & Society found that teens who are not on Facebook can be inadvertently excluded from social events. A fifteen-year-old girl who took part in the survey described how her performance group forgot to tell her that they were taking part in a school assembly. "No one remembered to tell me, because they had only posted it on Facebook," she said. "So after that I just got a Facebook [account] to know what's going on."[13]

Teens also use Facebook to carefully construct their public identities, and some spend a great deal of time editing or deleting past posts and managing which photographs of them are posted or tagged with their names. They often see the site as a reflection of their status and popularity, keeping close track of the number of "likes" their postings and photos receive. It is also easy to become enmeshed in gossip and drama, and many teens feel compelled to check the site frequently to see how conflicts play out. For those teens who have the

Many teens enjoy posting selfies and other photographs on their social media pages. Because these sites are easily accessed over smartphones, they can be managed and enjoyed at almost any time of day.

luxury of choosing their cell phones, their decision is often based on how well the phone interfaces with Facebook and other social media sites.

Gaps in Digital Interaction

While most teens say their cell phones are essential to maintaining normal social lives, some experts are concerned about how socializing in digital spaces—either by texting or on social media sites—is affecting today's youth. Amanda Lenhart explains that there is "a loss of cues in the digital world, e.g. tone of voice, body language, and all of the other non-verbal cues that we give robustly face-to-face that can sometimes prevent us from saying and doing very hurtful things."[14]

The lack of these cues is often the cause of misunderstandings, hurt feelings, and teen drama. Psychologist Michael Osit says, "I have many concerns about how much kids are relying on the inter-machine interaction in lieu of face to face socialization. How will they learn and practice the art of reading social nuances such as body language, physical and emotional boundaries, and other nonverbal messages if their relationship is based on . . . written messages consisting of two or three letter abbreviated words?"[15] Studies about how teens are actually affected are inconclusive, but Lenhart notes that the lack of cues often results in misunderstandings or hurt feelings, which is the cause of much of the teen drama that goes on in digital spaces.

> "Hours might have gone by between texts. As the receiver, silence can be deadly."[16]
>
> —*Therapist Donna Moss.*

The Downside of Constant Connection

Teens themselves sometimes feel as though they are a slave to their cell phones, which can beep and buzz every few minutes with social media updates and incoming texts. Many find it distracting, pulling them away from homework and sleep, and they wish they could step away from the constant interruptions. But as long as their friends are online, most teens feel they cannot tune out. One reason why teens feel compelled to respond is that it is expected. Though com-

Cell Phones and Family Time

When adolescents mature in a healthy way, their separation from their parents is gradual. As children get older, their peers have more and more influence on their attitudes and sense of identity. But parents still matter. Parents influence teens in areas like their education and career aspirations and help them navigate relationships. Peers, on the other hand, influence a teen's social identity, their likes and dislikes, and their hobbies and recreational activities. Experts believe that teens must have the influence of their parents as well as their peers to build healthy self-esteem and a healthy adult identity. When a teen is missing one of these domains of influence, he or she can have trouble with the maturing process and become overly dependent on either parents or peers.

Psychologist Suzanne Phillips thinks that the constant connection teens now have with their peers via cell phone is disrupting this balance. "Whereas coming home could mean alternative connections, impressions, and experiences with family members, the 24/7 cell phone connection precludes this," she writes. "It keeps a teen continually connected to peers but 'out of' the moment, place and relationships with parents and family." She suggests that families have set times when all cell phones are turned off—at the dinner table or during family activities—to restore the balance between parental and peer influence.

Suzanne Phillips, "Teens Sleeping with Cell Phones: A Clear and Present Danger," PBS. www.pbs.org.

municating on a cell phone does give them the option of delaying response or ignoring a message altogether, that action can be fraught with unintended meaning. Therapist Donna Moss sometimes sees this in her practice, when her teenaged clients bring in printed text messages to analyze. "Hours might have gone by between texts," she says. "As the receiver, silence can be deadly. Lost without cues or explanations, kids will go to extremes of assumptions and can lose a day of school work to this vast field of worry, rumination and attention deficit."[16]

Most teens have an unspoken agreement with at least some of their friends that they will respond to a text or other message promptly, and they expect the same courtesy in return. When there is silence, it can cause anxiety, distraction, and wounded feelings as the teen imagines the worst.

Texting and Romance

Communication by text is particularly unsuited for romantic relationships—yet teens still get to know each other, flirt, and even break up via text message. The influence of the cell phone on teen communication has also redefined many aspects of dating. For instance, if a teen says she is talking to someone—as in, she is interested in someone and they have not yet gone out on a date—there is a chance she means she has only met the person briefly (if at all) and is talking via text message. The casual nature of texting has also merged with the hook-up culture, in which teens go out in groups instead of on defined dates (and sometimes become casually intimate without first establishing that they are dating). For instance, a girl might text a boy telling him that she will see him later at a party and, because she said it in a text, feel no obligation to show up. Or a boy might send a girl suggestive text messages without having any intention of dating her. The flirting that goes on online or by text is sometimes referred to as a textationship, or a relationship based on text messages rather than face-to-face dating.

> "Digital communication is now firmly a part of teens' communicative arsenal."[18]
>
> —Amanda Lenhart, an expert on teens and technology.

While these relationships might sound trivial, to the young or inexperienced adolescent they can be both emotionally exhilarating and devastating. People engaging in these sorts of exchanges naturally fill in the blanks left by a lack of physical and verbal cues, and a teenager can mistakenly believe he or she is in an ideal relationship with an ideal mate—at least until communication breaks down. As Moss writes, "The person fails to respond for hours, during which time you basically go crazy with wonder, worry and then aggravation. There is, in essence, no way to interpret a stone wall of silence."[17]

Critical for Social Development

For good or for ill, the cell phone is now a critical part of a teenager's social development. Most teens feel empowered by their cell phones, and they enjoy the way their phones improve their connection to their loved ones. At the same time, they can become overwhelmed by the demands their cell phones—and their social networks—make on them. However, opting out of cell phone ownership is not a realistic choice for most teens; those who do not own a cell phone find it increasingly difficult to develop and maintain a healthy social life. As Lenhart notes, "Digital communication is now firmly a part of teens' communicative arsenal."[18] And while communication via cell phone has its problems, it is now the centerpiece of a healthy teenage social life.

Cell Phones and Addiction

Chapter Two

In its 24 Hours: Unplugged experiment, the International Center for Media and the Public Agenda asked two hundred undergraduates at the University of Maryland to go on a media fast. They were to abstain from using all media and mobile technologies for a single day. Most found this extremely difficult to do—so difficult that many simply could not last the full twenty-four hours. The technology that was hardest to do without was the cell phone, which the students used primarily to keep in touch with their friends and family via text message and on social networking sites like Facebook and Twitter. Without their phones, most students felt so cut off and alone that they were unable to function. When they described their experiences afterward, many used the language of addiction—they were "in withdrawal," "frantically craving," "very anxious," "jittery," and "miserable."[19] As one participant admitted, "I clearly am addicted and the dependency is sickening."[20]

These reactions should be no surprise to any teenager with a cell phone who has been unable to resist the ping of an incoming message—even if it happens at the dinner table, in the middle of the night, or while driving. A cell phone is the tool teens use to connect with their friends and family, and they do so in a myriad of ways: they text, tweet, e-mail, post pictures and videos, and comment on the minute-to-minute updates that appear on their social networking sites. It is no wonder that a study at Stanford University found that 94 percent of participants felt some level of addiction to their iPhones, with 44 percent of them ranking their addiction level as a four or five on a five-point scale.

Are Cell Phones Addictive?

Still, there is debate among experts about whether or not cell phones—and the Internet most of them access—are actually addictive. Addiction is a complicated concept that still is not well defined among scientists. Some experts think that substance addictions like alcoholism and behavioral addictions like compulsive gambling are essentially the same thing—a dysfunction of the reward circuitry of the brain—and that cell phone and Internet addictions should be treated like substance addictions. Others believe that behavioral addictions do not really exist; they are just symptoms of underlying mental disorders like depression or obsessive-compulsive disorder (OCD). In the newly revised *Diagnostic and Statistical Manual of Mental Disorders* (DSM-5), the definitive handbook of mental disorders published by the American Psychiatric Association, the only behavioral addiction that is included is gambling disorder. Internet addiction disorder does not appear, even though hundreds of peer-reviewed studies have described the condition since 1995, when the term was first coined, and more and more mental health professionals are specializing in treating the disorder.

"I clearly am addicted and the dependency is sickening."[20]

—University of Maryland student.

Internet addiction disorder can involve many different activities—from shopping to viewing pornography. Teenagers tend to overindulge in two activities that happen to be well suited for the cell phone: texting and social networking. While some might say that teens are on their phones so much because they like to socialize, new research is suggesting that something more might be going on.

Dopamine and the Compulsion Loop

To understand how texting and social networking can become addictive, it is useful to first examine the most prominent Internet addiction, Internet gaming disorder. Most people are familiar with how addictive computer games can be, but since the early 2000s, game designers have been using scientific insights about the brain to deliberately make their games as addictive as possible. Neuroscientists have discovered that when rewards are frequent but unpredictable, the brain releases dopamine. Dopamine is a neurotransmitter that affects salience, or what we consider to be important at any given moment. Dopamine does not just make us feel good; it makes us pay attention

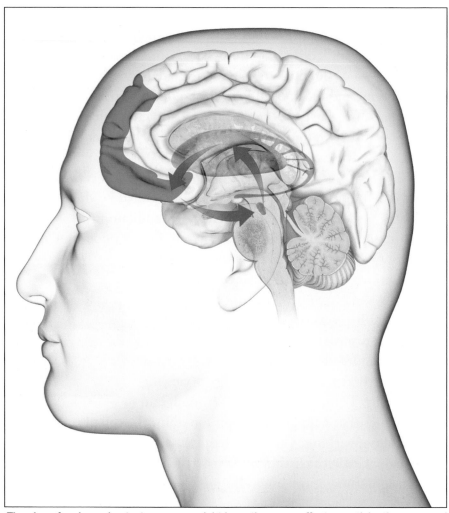

The ping of an incoming text message might have the same effect as anticipating a reward in a video game. In both cases the feeling of anticipation is caused by the release of dopamine, which flows (as indicated by the arrows) in the pleasure center of the brain.

to things that have made us feel good in the past. When people anticipate good feelings—whether that is a win at a casino game, a hit of nicotine from a cigarette, or an e-mail from a loved one—that feeling of anticipation, or craving, is caused by the release of dopamine. Dopamine makes people feel compelled to act: to gamble, light up, or check their cell phone for a new message.

When computer game designers integrate this knowledge into their game design, they create what is called a compulsion loop.

The goal of any compulsion loop is to keep people playing the game as long as possible and to make them return again and again. *Farmville*, a popular game that can be played within Facebook, creates compulsion loops by doling out small rewards over time as players build and tend their farms. It also gives players surprise rewards at unpredictable times, which heightens the dopamine response. Game designer Andrea Phillips describes compulsion loops in this way: "It's that tension of knowing you might get the treat, but not knowing exactly when, that keeps you playing. The player develops an unshakeable faith, after a while, that THIS will be the time I hit it big."[21]

Dopamine and Texting

The compulsion loops that game designers create (by doling out small rewards often but at unpredictable times) happen to mimic the flow of information that comes through a cell phone. Researchers suspect that hearing the ping of an incoming message can have the same effect as anticipating a reward in a game. As Bill Davidow writes in the *Atlantic*, "We now believe that the compulsion to continually check email, stock prices, and sporting scores on smartphones is driven in some cases by dopamine releases that occur in anticipation of receiving good news."[22] Even though that good news might only be a response to a text from a friend or an interesting piece of gossip on Facebook, it is because these rewards are both frequent and unpredictable that dopamine is released.

> "Neuro-imaging has shown that back and forth texting floods the pleasure centers of the brain, the same area that lights up when using heroin."[23]
>
> —Psychologist Suzanne Phillips.

And as psychologist Suzanne Phillips explains, the news does not have to be good to affect dopamine. "Neuro-imaging has shown that back and forth texting floods the pleasure centers of the brain, the same area that lights up when using heroin. The emotional disruption of a real or perceived negative response, however, necessitates more texting to repair the mood, to fix the feelings of rejection, blame and disconnection. The addictive potential is obvious."[23]

All About Me

Researchers have also learned that self-disclosure—or talking about oneself—is intrinsically rewarding to human beings. A 2012 study found that when people answer questions about themselves, the reward center of the brain is more active than when they answer questions about other people. The study's authors write, "We suggest that humans so willingly self-disclose because doing so represents an event with intrinsic value, in the same way as with primary rewards such as food and sex."[24] Participants in the 2012 study were also willing to give up a monetary reward for the opportunity to answer questions about themselves—especially if another person was listening.

This helps explain the popularity of social networking sites, where it is estimated that 80 percent of all posts are about what the poster is thinking or experiencing—in other words, self-disclosure. It also explains the compulsion to check messages frequently. When teenagers disclose something about themselves—either in a social network post or a text message—they feel far more anticipation as they wait for the response than they do if they are, for instance, waiting for a friend to text them the latest homework assignment. Their dopamine response, and therefore their urge to check their phone, is stronger.

The Lure of Drama

Text messaging and social networking encourage self-disclosure, dole out small rewards in the form of messages and responses, and deliver those rewards in an unpredictable manner—all of which is enough to keep a teenager focused on his or her phone. The final piece of the addiction puzzle is the nature of many of the texts, tweets, and posts that circulate through a teenager's social network. Drama—the gossip, verbal sparring, and angst that goes on at every high school—is commonly the topic of teen conversation and therefore the topic of many text messages. And drama absolutely thrives on social networking sites like Facebook, especially because postings contain no voice or body language cues to convey the authors' intent and therefore can be easily misconstrued. It is also much easier to say inflammatory things in a Facebook post than face-to-face, where good manners—or fear of reprisal—tend to keep people respectful.

A Fake Disorder

Internet addiction disorder started as a hoax. In 1995 psychologist Ivan Goldberg made up a fake disorder whose sufferers had symptoms such as "fantasies or dreams about the Internet" and "voluntary or involuntary typing movements of the fingers" to parody the complexity of the *Diagnostic and Statistical Manual of Mental Disorders*. After he posted the disorder on an online bulletin board, other psychologists claiming to have problems with excessive Internet use began to contact him for help. Goldberg was alarmed that his parody had been taken at face value. "To medicalize every behavior by putting it into psychiatric nomenclature is ridiculous," he explained to the *New Yorker*. "If you expand the concept of addiction to include everything people can overdo, then you must talk about people being addicted to books, addicted to jogging, addicted to other people." Despite its beginnings, many psychiatrists and therapists began to specialize in studying and treating Internet addiction disorder as more and more people found that they were unable to disconnect from their computers.

Quoted in David Wallis, "Just Click No," *New Yorker*, January 13, 1997. www.newyorker.com.

Many teens complain about all the drama on Facebook and claim to be moving away from the platform for that reason. However, following drama as it unfolds can be riveting, and the need to know what happens next can be consuming. It is the reason that soap operas, and now reality shows, are so popular; they glorify conflict between the participants. But what is even more compelling for teens is following a conflict online between people they know—or being enmeshed in the conflict themselves. Everyone wants to know how stories end, especially when that story is about oneself.

The Signs of Cell Phone Addiction

Doctors frequently use questionnaires to assess whether or not a person is addicted to a substance or a behavior. So far, no scale that measures cell phone addiction has been officially accepted in the scientific community. However, several have been developed and are commonly used, such as the Cell Phone Overuse Scale. This scale is based on the scale used to diagnose gambling disorder, the only behavioral addiction included in the DSM. Its twenty-four questions cover areas like increased use over time, inability to cut back on use because of withdrawal symptoms like anxiety, and engaging in the behavior despite risks and negative consequences. Being unable to stop a behavior despite negative consequences—like getting in an automobile accident or failing in school because of excessive texting—is the hallmark of any addiction.

Though anyone can spend too much time on a cell phone, researchers have found that people who are either impulsive or materialistic tend to overuse their cell phone. In a study of 191 college students, researchers James Roberts and Stephen Pirog found that students who had a hard time exercising self-control or who valued expensive objects tended to score the highest in cell phone overuse. Impulsivity is a trait common to most people who suffer from addictions, from alcoholism to compulsive shopping. But people who are materialistic tend to use objects—like a cell phone—to heighten their own status. Roberts explained that when people use their phone excessively in public, "we're signaling that we've got this shiny object, this status symbol, our iPhone or Android or Blackberry, and that we've got important people to talk to or text, who are maybe even more important than the people right in front of us. And that we're so important that we have to talk everywhere and all the time in front of others."[25]

Sleeping with a Cell Phone

Another hallmark of cell phone overuse among teens is using the phone throughout the night. In a survey by the Pew Research Center, more than 80 percent of teens said they slept with their phones. For most people cell phones have taken the place of clocks and alarms, so having a phone by the bedside is understandable. However, many teens feel pressured to be available to their friends via text at all times and do not mute their phones. "People will wake me up in the middle of the night and I have to wake up and talk or they will think I'm mad

Teens who feel pressured to be available to friends at all times often end up sleeping with their phones to avoid missing texts or social media postings. By disrupting their sleep this way, teens put their health and well-being at risk.

at them or something,"[26] a teenager told PBS. Others will continue texting or social networking long into the night and eventually become sleep deprived.

Therapist Donna Moss says that she sees a pervasive pattern in her teenage clients: They are texting until one or two o'clock in the morning and wake up exhausted and late for school. Then, she

Gaming Addiction

Computer games have always inspired obsession. But the rise of massively multiplayer online games in the late 1990s and early 2000s brought people's obsession with gaming to a whole new level. Psychiatrist Jerald J. Block, who has been treating Internet addiction for years, believes online gamers are the hardest to treat. S. Craig Watkins interviewed Block for his book *The Young and the Digital.* He writes, "Block has . . . treated patients who could not pull themselves away from their computers long enough to take a shower. Others have lost their jobs or friends from the overuse of a virtual world. Some of Block's patients even admit to setting up toilets near their computers so that they can remain close to their online friends."

Gaming addiction is not just a problem in the United States; Asian countries like South Korea, China, and Taiwan consider gaming addiction to be a grave national problem. At least ten people have died in those countries from blood clots, which form in the legs if a person sits in one position for too long; the clots can then travel to the heart, lungs, or brain. And in a tragic incident in South Korea, a young couple allowed their infant daughter to die from malnutrition while they raised a virtual child online in a nearby Internet café.

Quoted in S. Craig Watkins, *The Young and the Digital.* Boston: Beacon, 2009, p. 134.

says, "they complain of feeling depressed and anxious much of the time, out of control, OCD, anorexic. And, how do they typically self-soothe this kind of pressure? . . . more texting and going to bed late, plus energy drinks . . . a vicious cycle of self-induced mental fatigue."[27] Research has shown that teenagers need nine hours of sleep each night, and if they become sleep deprived they can develop memory problems, reduced concentration and creativity, and even anxiety and depressive disorders.

Can Cell Phones Change the Brain?

There is a growing school of thought that the shift to digital media is causing significant changes in the ability to process information. People's attention spans seem to be getting shorter, and their self-control seems to be weakening. "There's little doubt we're becoming more impulsive,"[28] explains psychiatrist Elias Aboujaoude, who runs the Obsessive Compulsive Disorder Clinic and Impulse Control Disorders Clinic at Stanford University School of Medicine. He notes that since the Internet has become pervasive in daily life, rates of OCD and attention-deficit/hyperactivity disorder (ADHD) in the population are increasing. In fact, ADHD diagnoses have increased by 66 percent over the last ten years. Aboujaoude sees a direct cause and effect between the pervasiveness of technology and impulsive and addictive behavior. "There's just something about the medium that's addictive," he says about digital technology. "I've seen plenty of patients who have no history of addictive behavior—or substance abuse of any kind—become addicted via the Internet and these other technologies."[29]

The reason may be that the digital medium is changing our brains. Nicholas Carr, author of *The Shallows: What the Internet Is Doing to Our Brains*, believes that the way people read and write on their digital devices makes it increasingly difficult for them to process in-depth information. He first noticed this problem in himself, when he realized that reading more than a page or two caused him to fidget and drift. "But my brain, I realized, wasn't just drifting," he recalls. "It was hungry. It was demanding to be fed the way the Net fed it— and the more it was fed, the hungrier it became. Even when I was away from my computer, I yearned to check e-mail, click links, do some Googling. I wanted to be *connected*."[30]

The brain, he goes on to explain, changes depending on what it experiences, rewiring itself to master whatever activity it is exposed to on a regular basis. Therefore, if it is constantly exposed to a medium where information is presented in short bursts, filled with hyperlinks and distractions, it will become adept at that sort of processing. Carr discusses one study by research company nGenera of six thousand teenagers who grew up with digital technology. It turns out that many of them did not always read from left to right and top to bottom; instead, they skipped around, looking for information

> "Even when I was away from my computer, I yearned to check e-mail, click links, do some Googling. I wanted to be *connected*."[30]
>
> —Nicholas Carr, author of The Shallows: What the Internet Is Doing to Our Brains.

that interested them. This ability of the brain to rewire itself is called neuroplasticity, and it is a component of both learning and addiction. "As particular circuits in our brain strengthen through the repetition of a physical or mental activity," Carr writes, "they begin to transform that activity into a habit."[31] The current habits of teens—to use their cell phones to constantly cultivate and monitor their minute-by-minute connection to others and to the digital landscape—may well be a result of this neuroplasticity in action. The problem is that once the brain rewires itself, it resists changes, and a person suddenly feels addicted.

Can the Brain Heal Itself?

Luckily, there is hope for those who feel they cannot live without their cell phones. Experts suggest that teens who feel overwhelmed by being constantly available to everyone in their social network create a new habit by carving out a few hours from each day to be phone-free. Using that time to read a book or a long article will help train the brain to process in-depth information. Spending time in a natural setting also can help restore the brain. "After spending time in a quiet rural setting, close to nature, people exhibit greater attentiveness, stronger memory, and generally improved cognition. Their brains become both calmer and sharper,"[32] Carr writes. Neuroplasticity works both ways, and with a little effort, the brain can be restored to its preaddicted state.

Texting While Driving

Chapter Three

The night before Mariah West's high school graduation, she hopped into her car and headed off to watch an acquaintance play baseball. She was not sure where she was going, so while she was driving he texted her directions. When she looked down to read one of his messages, her car veered off the highway, crossed the grassy median, and crashed into a concrete bridge abutment. She died at the hospital. The text she had been reading said, "Where u at."

Mariah's story is featured in the award-winning documentary *The Last Text*, produced as part of the It Can Wait campaign, an effort by AT&T and three other major cell phone providers to educate their customers about the consequences of texting and driving. The campaign asks both teens and adults to take a pledge to stop texting while driving, and it seems to be making an impact in high schools across the country. "When we show them the documentary," Merry Dye, Mariah's mother, says, "[the students] cover their mouths in that classic view of horror. They get it."[33] The short film was created by award-winning filmmaker Werner Herzog, who also created a thirty-minute documentary on the same subject titled *From One Second to the Next*. As of November 2013, that film has been viewed on YouTube almost 2.5 million times. "If one single accident because of that film will be prevented," Herzog told the *Los Angeles Times*, "I can be proud."[34]

What Is Distracted Driving?

For a teen who compulsively or excessively texts, getting a driver's license can be a death sentence. The Insurance Institute for Highway Safety Fatality Facts estimates that eleven teenagers die every day from texting while driving. Drivers who text are twenty-three times more likely to be involved in an automobile crash than drivers who are not distracted. The National Safety Council estimates that at least 28 percent of all automobile accidents—or at least 1.6 million accidents each year—involve drivers who are distracted by their cell phones.

Texting while driving is a type of behavior that experts have dubbed distracted driving. Distracted driving includes more activities than talking or texting on a cell phone. It can include eating and drinking, talking to a passenger, reading a map, putting on makeup, or even reacting to an insect inside the car. According to the Centers for Disease Control and Prevention (CDC), there are three types of distraction: taking your eyes off the road, taking your hands off the wheel, and taking your mind off driving. Texting while driving is particularly dangerous because it encompasses all three types of distraction. On average, sending or receiving a text takes a driver's eyes off the road for 4.6 seconds. At 55 miles an hour (89 kph), that is equivalent to driving the length of a football field blindfolded.

More Dangerous than Drunk Driving

Historically, alcohol-related car accidents have always been the leading cause of death among teenagers of driving age. However, this changed in 2013, when a study by Cohen Children's Medical Center found that texting has passed drunk driving as the leading cause of death among teenagers. Three thousand to four thousand teenagers die in texting-related accidents each year, compared to twenty-seven hundred teens who die in drunk-driving accidents. Andrew Adesman, who conducted the study, was not surprised. "The reality is kids aren't drinking seven days per week—they are carrying their phones and texting seven days per week, so you intuitively know this a more common occurrence,"[35] he told CBS News. The results of the study were supported by a *Car and Driver* experiment that showed that drivers took longer to hit the brakes if they were distracted by reading a text than if they were under the influence of alcohol.

To make matters worse, teens who text and drive are also more likely to engage in other risky behavior. A national Youth Risk Behavior Survey found that teens who text and drive are less likely to wear their seat belt regularly, twice as likely to ride with a driver who has been drinking, and five times as likely to drink and drive as teens who say they do not text while driving. They are also more likely to binge drink, smoke tobacco, use marijuana, and have unsafe sex. "It's

32

Texting while driving has become a major hazard on city streets and highways. Texting drivers are far more likely to be involved in an automobile crash than drivers who are not distracted.

not surprising that kids who take such risks in one area may be more likely to take risks in other areas,"[36] said Thomas Frieden, director of the CDC.

Texting While Driving at Night

Driving at night has always been more dangerous for inexperienced drivers because visibility is reduced and drivers are more likely to be tired. About half of all teen crash fatalities happen at night. However, as cell phone use increases, the proportion of nighttime fatalities has increased as well. Before teenagers carried cell phones, about 45 percent of fatal crashes involving teens occurred at night. By 2008 the percentage of fatal crashes that happened at night rose by 10 percent.

Experts like Bernie Fette, senior research specialist for the Texas Transportation Institute, attribute this increase to texting while driving. Fette explains that part of the problem is that many teens do not think it is more risky to drive at night, so they continue to text as often as they do in the daytime. A survey of twenty thousand teen drivers revealed that only 3 percent thought driving at night was a risk factor. "We have talked to a lot of kids who say, 'Look, it's not that difficult. I can text in my pocket,'" Fette said. "But being comfortable with technology doesn't add security when you use it in an environment where it creates danger."[37]

Texting While Driving and ADHD

Another factor that makes texting more dangerous is having a diagnosis of ADHD. The CDC estimates that about 6.4 million young people have received a diagnosis of ADHD at some point in their lives. The hallmarks of the disorder are problems with concentration and impulse control. Unfortunately, these problems put teens who have ADHD at particular risk as new drivers. About 17 percent of teenagers with ADHD have received one or more traffic tickets, whereas only 6 percent of teens without ADHD have been ticketed.

> "We have talked to a lot of kids who say, 'Look, it's not that difficult. I can text in my pocket.'"[37]
>
> —Bernie Fette, transportation specialist.

Jeffery Epstein, director of the Center for ADHD at Cincinnati Children's Hospital Medical Center in Ohio, wanted to find out if texting and driving is more dangerous for teens with ADHD. He recruited sixty-one drivers between the ages of sixteen and seventeen, about half of whom had ADHD. The teens operated a driving simulator, first with no distractions, and then while talking and then texting with a researcher. When there were no distractions, the teens with ADHD were worse drivers than the control group, straying outside of their lanes about 1.8 percent of the time. However, when texting, both sets of teens had significant problems. Teens without ADHD were suddenly driving as if they had the disorder, straying out of their lanes 2 percent of the time. And teens with ADHD almost doubled their driving problems, straying out of their lanes 3.3 percent of the time. "That's just a heck of a lot of time for a kid or any driver to be out of their lane when they're driving,"[38] Epstein said.

Andrew Adesman, chief of developmental and behavioral pediatrics at Cohen Children's Medical Center, has studied ways to help

The New York Solution

While there may seem to be no way to prevent teens from texting behind the wheel, Governor Andrew Cuomo of New York believes he has a solution. Thirty-nine states and the District of Columbia have laws against texting while driving, but most of them are ineffective because offenders are rarely caught, and when they are, they simply have to pay a fine. However, on July 1, 2013, Cuomo signed a law that treats texting while driving (and other forms of distracted driving) like reckless driving. Teenagers with learner's permits or junior licenses will lose their license for sixty days if they are caught, which law enforcement officials in New York believe will be an effective deterrent. Other drivers will get high fines and five points against their licenses.

teens with and without ADHD improve their driving. "The deficit that kids with ADHD seem to have is that they tend to let their eyes look away from the roadway for longer glances than do experienced drivers,"[39] Adesman explained. He believes that teens would improve if they were aware of how long they were looking away from the road. Eye-tracking systems that sound an alarm when teens look away from the windshield for more than two seconds at a time may help teens self-correct, he said. Unfortunately, this technology is not yet commercially available.

Are Teens Just Risk Takers?

Even though almost all teens claim they understand the risks, many teens still text and drive. Survey results vary; one study found that 43 percent of all high school students who drive admit to texting while driving. Another study found that a whopping 78 percent of teens admitted to texting behind the wheel. Unfortunately, texting while driving is not an occasional occurrence; one-quarter of teens say they respond to a text message at least once every time they drive.

It is still not clear why teens are taking these risks. Even though most have been exposed to national education and awareness programs and understand the dangers, teenagers are still texting behind the wheel as often as ever. The authors of a study in *Pediatrics* speculate that teens who take these risks may "perceive greater emotional and social rewards associated with the behaviors"[40] than teens who do not take such risks.

The rewards may simply be social acceptance. Not answering a text immediately is considered rude, and almost all teens expect a response within five minutes. "I've seen it firsthand," says Randye Hoder in a *New York Times* editorial. "My son gets antsy when I tell him he cannot return a text to a friend while we are at the family dinner table. And when I tell him not to respond to a text while we are midconversation, he furrows his brow and looks at me as if to say it is inconceivable for him not to answer."[41] Hoder was prompted to write the editorial when her son, Nathanial, reached for his phone during a practice driving session. "If he went for his phone with me right there," Hoder wondered, "what would he do when he had his license and I was no longer in the car, watching his every move?"[42]

> "That's just a heck of a lot of time for a kid or any driver to be out of their lane."[38]
>
> —Jeffery Epstein, director of the Center for ADHD at Cincinnati Children's Hospital Medical Center in Ohio.

A second theory the authors of the *Pediatrics* study propose is that these risk-taking teens may believe that texting while driving only once in a while—when the message is very important, for instance, or when traffic is light—carries very little risk and is therefore worth it. This belief—that just once will not hurt—tends to be a rationalization people use to justify impulsive behavior. It is therefore possible that teens who make this justification to themselves simply have poor impulse control. Poor impulse control is a hallmark of compulsive behavior, such as hypertexting (sending more than 120 text messages per school day) or binge drinking. But it is also a part of adolescence. Teens who know it is dangerous but do it anyway may just be acting normally for their age.

Are Parents Poor Role Models?

Because education efforts and laws prohibiting texting while driving have done little to reduce the incidence of the problem among teenagers, some experts are concluding that parents have the best chance of stopping the behavior. The problem is that adults use their cell phones behind the wheel, too. Even though texting while driving is more dangerous for teenagers because they have less experience behind the wheel, far more adults get into texting-related accidents than teenagers do. "Texting while driving is not just a teen problem," said John Ulczycki of the National Safety Council. "Teens text. But you're looking

High school students in Albuquerque, New Mexico, sign a no-texting pledge board in 2013 as part of AT&T's "It Can Wait" campaign urging young people to avoid texting while driving. An AT&T survey revealed, however, that adult drivers are even more likely than teen drivers to text behind the wheel.

A Tragedy in Missouri

On May 16, 2013, sixteen-year-old Savannah Nash of Harrisonville, Missouri, took her very first solo drive in the family's PT Cruiser. She had only gotten her license a week before, and her parents gave her permission to go to the store alone to pick up something for dinner. At 4:10 p.m., just a short distance from her house, she pulled onto Missouri Highway 7 but did not see the tractor-trailer heading toward her at high speed. Her vehicle was hit on the driver's side and carried by the truck across the median and into the opposite lane. Though Nash was wearing her seat belt, she was killed on impact. The police believe that Nash was distracted by her cell phone, which contained a long text message that she had composed but not yet sent.

at around 10 million teen drivers, but about 180 million other adult drivers."[43] The percentage of adults who text behind the wheel may be higher as well. As part of its It Can Wait campaign, AT&T surveyed 1,011 drivers and found that, even though 98 percent of adult drivers knew texting and driving is dangerous, almost 50 percent of them still did it, compared to 43 percent of teenagers.

There is also evidence that even when an adult becomes a parent, he or she keeps on texting behind the wheel. Many parents who tell their teens not to text and drive do it themselves—and right in front of their kids. A recent survey found that 59 percent of teens have seen their parents text and drive, and 91 percent have seen their parents talking on the phone while driving. "Kids begin to learn to drive long before we think they do," said Dave Melton, director of Transportation Technical Consulting Services at the Liberty Mutual Research Institute for Safety. "They go to the driving school of mom and dad for a long, long time. How can we expect them to do anything other than what we've taught them?"[44]

Can Technology Solve the Problem?

Currently, the best chance society has to curb texting and other cell phone use behind the wheel is technological interventions—

applications that can be installed on a cell phone that take away a driver's choice and make texting while driving impossible. Several smartphone applications are currently on the market. Most of them lock the phone while the car is in motion, either by using the motion-sensing and GPS technology inside the cell phone or by interfacing with the car's computer. One such application, iZup (pronounced "eyes up"), goes a step further by sending incoming calls to voice mail and allowing 911 calls. Another application, Cellcontrol, is available for free to teenaged customers of the online car insurance company Esurance. Several other applications allow parents to monitor their teen driver's speed and texting habits and let them know if the application has been deleted or tampered with. The state of Iowa is even developing its own phone-locking application called TXTL8R, which it will offer free to teenaged drivers and their parents.

There is some evidence that parents may resist installing these types of devices on their children's cell phones. Researchers recruited eighty-four newly licensed teenaged drivers for a study that installed devices in their vehicles that let their parents monitor their driving habits. The researchers had a hard time recruiting enough participants for the study, however. As the study's authors wrote, "Parents who declined to participate usually said their teenagers opposed it, or they were concerned about intruding on the privacy of their children or jeopardizing trust with them."[45] Also, two-thirds of the teens who did participate in the study admitted to trying to drown out the devices' alerts with music. Experts concluded that monitoring devices probably would not solve the texting while driving problem because most parents simply would not install the devices. A similar study found that only 32 to 51 percent of parents surveyed would consider installing a monitoring device, even if it helped keep their teen safe. To date, no studies have looked at how widespread smartphone locking applications are, but many experts are skeptical about whether they will gain in popularity.

"If he went for his phone with me right there, what would he do when he had his license and I was no longer in the car, watching his every move?"[42]

—Randye Hoder, mother of a teen driver.

A Powerful Addiction

Texting while driving is the most potentially devastating symptom of compulsive cell phone use. Unfortunately, it often happens while other teenagers are in the car—which is yet another source of distraction. The fact that teens are aware of the dangers but still are unable to curb their cell phone use while driving illustrates how powerfully addictive a cell phone can be. Ultimately, a technological innovation, such as improving the technology behind hands-free cell phone operation, might be the only way to solve the problem.

Oversharing and Sexting

Chapter Four

On an episode of the MTV show *Catfish*, Jenn, a teenager from Iowa, has fallen in love online with a boy named Skylar. Though they have been talking and texting for eight months, Skylar will not video chat with her, let alone meet her in person. Jenn, who is suspicious, asks the show's host, Nev Schulman, to help her find out if Skylar is real. He is not; his name is Bryan, and he has been lying to a string of young women—Jenn included—to hone his dating skills. Jenn is crushed. She has been fooled by a catfish, a slang term for a person who pursues an online relationship by pretending to be someone they are not.

What caused Jenn to get herself in this situation is called the online disinhibition effect. First described by psychologist John Suler, the term refers to the way people tend to lose their inhibitions online, or "self-disclose or act out more frequently or intensely than they would in person."[46] Disinhibition makes people like Jenn able to drop their guard and become emotionally intimate with strangers. Normal social conventions are either absent or not enforced online, which allows people to feel much freer than they do in society. This is not necessarily negative; in fact, it is a boon to shy or introverted people—especially teenagers—who can try out different aspects of their personalities in relative safety. Teens who might be too shy to make friends or flirt because they are afraid of rejection can use the anonymity and invisibility of the online world to protect themselves while they reach out. The Internet can be a place where deep friendships are formed. And with the popularity of the cell phone, real-life relationships can be strengthened, deepened, and cultivated through constant contact.

But disinhibition can also provide a false sense of safety and security. Texting can feel private and intimate, and it is easy to forget that texts can be copied, saved, shared, and posted online. Facebook and other social networking sites can also feel private, and it is easy to forget who has access to posts—or to make a mistake when configuring privacy settings. And now that most cell phones have a camera, a video recorder, and access to a variety of powerful search engines online, anyone can share anything in an instant. Compulsive sharing can lead to large errors in judgment. As psychologist Jeremy Dean, the author of *PsyBlog*, explains, "The online disinhibition effect has cost people their jobs, their income and their relationships, yet many are still oblivious to it."[47]

Oversharing

Scott Fitzsimones got his first iPhone on his thirteenth birthday. As he told the *Washington Post*, he immediately set up a Facebook account and started downloading apps from iTunes. Within a few minutes, he had given away a lot of personal information: Facebook knew his name, his birthday, and where he went to school; iTunes had his family's full names, their e-mail addresses, and their credit card number; and many of the apps he downloaded could trace his exact location with GPS technology. "The first time he was asked to share his location on the game Pocket God, the seventh-grader paused for a moment to consider why the company would want to know his whereabouts," Cecilia Kang writes. "But he feared that if he didn't agree, his experience on the app would be limited. . . . So he tapped 'okay,' feeling comfort in the masses; his friends, after all, were using the app and never complained."[48]

> "The online disinhibition effect has cost people their jobs, their income and their relationships."[47]
>
> —Psychologist Jeremy Dean.

Even though many kids like Fitzsimones are in the midst of puberty and the decision-making parts of their brains are still under development, they are treated like adults on the Internet when it comes to privacy. Privacy laws usually apply to kids up to twelve years old. And thirteen is the age of consent for joining most social networking sites, including Facebook. Legislators and advocates are concerned that kids are giving away too much information online, putting themselves at risk for fraud, identity theft, and stalking by pedophiles. The cybersecurity company Lifelock recently surveyed seven hundred teens aged thirteen to seventeen and found that three out of four overshare personal information. Twenty-nine percent said they share their full date of birth, 23 percent share part of their home address, and 63 percent share the name of their school.

Another cybersecurity company, Trend Micro, reported that teens were posting pictures of their first credit card or their new driver's license on social networking sites. "Cybercriminals will only need to do a simple search on Instagram and Twitter," Trend Micro explains, "and they can get hold of a lot of sensitive information, which they can use to purchase items, initiate transactions, cover their tracks, etc."[49]

"My Stupid Picture Won't Die"

The intrinsic pleasure of sharing personal information combined with the disinhibition effect and the anticipation of getting positive feedback from peers online tempts many teens to share information and pictures that can come back to haunt them later. Parents sometimes find out their teenager was drinking or smoking marijuana by finding pictures online. A youth journalism program at the University of

Teens who post photos on social media sites showing them partying or in other potentially compromising settings may regret it later. Colleges, employers, and others often check such sites when making admissions and hiring decisions.

The Sexting App

Snapchat, a popular messaging application, allows the user to snap a picture and immediately send it with a caption to another Snapchat user. It is appealing because ten seconds after the message is received, the picture deletes itself completely from the receiver's device. Teens often use Snapchat for texting, taking pictures of their faces and using them in place of emoticons.

Because of this unique feature, Snapchat has become known as "the sexting app." Teens use the application to send each other nude or sexually explicit images, with the understanding that the image will self-destruct in a few seconds. However, users have found a way to take a screen shot of images sent through Snapchat and save them. Several instances of boys taking screen shots of sexts and then forwarding them to their friends have made the national news. One took place in 2013 in Ridgewood, New Jersey, where two teen girls found their topless "selfies" posted on Instagram. Police got involved and gave everyone involved a short amnesty period to delete the images.

Snapchat recently announced that it is adding the ability to send short videos. It also now warns people in its iTunes description that images can be saved if the receiver takes a screen shot.

Saint Thomas in Minnesota has created a website called Protect My Rep, which tries to educate teenagers about how to protect their online reputations. On the site, a teenager named Elizabeth shares her story of a seminude picture she posted on Facebook as a joke. Even though she quickly deleted it, when she got to school the next day she discovered that the picture had been saved and forwarded to everyone. "My stupid picture won't die,"[50] Elizabeth said, and she knows it is still out there to this day.

These kinds of missteps can follow teens for years, affecting their ability to join the military or get a job. "You wouldn't want to be seen on Facebook as attacking someone's character. That seems like a red flag to employers," Erik Aamoth, a workforce center manager, explains. He says that employers seeing such a post wonder,

"Are they going to be the person who comes to my office and causes trouble?"[51]

Oversharing can also affect a teenager's chances of getting into college. College admissions officers often check a prospective student's online presence. A survey from Kaplan Test Prep found that 31 percent of colleges said they often browse a student's social media pages during the admissions process—usually to follow up on something included in an application, like an award. However, about a third of them said they had come across negative information, like evidence of underage alcohol use, which affected the student's chance of acceptance.

The *New York Times* reported that a high school student who was attending a college information session at Bowdoin College apparently tweeted disparaging comments about the students around her while the presentation was going on. An admissions officer found out about it because Bowdoin regularly tracks mentions of the college on Twitter and elsewhere. The girl did not get into Bowdoin because her academic record was not good enough, but even if it had been, she still may have been rejected. "We would have wondered about the judgment of someone who spends their time on their mobile phone and makes such awful remarks,"[52] the dean of admissions told *New York Times* writer Natasha Singer. Singer expresses concern that this practice may be a violation of privacy.

> "You wouldn't want to be seen on Facebook as attacking someone's character. That seems like a red flag to employers."[51]
>
> —Erik Aamoth, workforce center manager.

Are Teens Really So Clueless?

Will Oremus does not share Singer's concern. In an article in *Slate* magazine, he argues that today's teenagers are aware that posts made to public sites are just that—public—and that there is nothing worrisome about Bowdoin reading the high school student's tweets. "That's not akin to snooping on the young woman's private diary," he writes. "It's more like noticing that she's shouting expletives at passersby while standing in the middle of the quad."[53] He notes that many teens understand this so well that they have two Facebook accounts—a public one for the world to see and a private one, often kept secret from their parents, for their friends. A survey by the Pew Research Center found that teens are aware of online privacy issues; only 17 percent of teens have their privacy settings set to public on their social media sites, and 55 percent say they have made the deliberate decision not to publish content that might come back to haunt them in the future. Senior research specialist Amanda Lenhart says, "I think youth absolutely care about their privacy and take steps to protect it."[54]

In fact, many teens are more savvy about how to maintain privacy than are adults who work in the information technology field. Jacqui Cheng, editor of the technology website Ars Technica, wrote about her experience teaching a six-week summer program that introduced inner-city Chicago teenagers to careers in technology.

> "I felt like if I didn't do it, they wouldn't continue to talk to me."[58]
>
> —A teenager who was pressured into sexting nude pictures of herself to boys.

Cheng was surprised that the teens—many of whom had smartphones—were more knowledgeable about privacy and social media than her colleagues. She even learned new privacy techniques from the teens, like their practice of deleting an entire Facebook account instead of just logging out. Since Facebook keeps account information online, the teens would simply reactivate their account every time they went online. This kept out nosey parents and school officials. Cheng said, "I came from a world where everyone believes the kids are the ones who have no clue. Instead, the kids were the ones asking me why any person with a brain would let their phone attach a GPS location to a photograph's EXIF file [a hidden information file that is attached to a photo]."[55] Cheng said that her students were only posting information they wanted people to see, carefully crafting their online identities.

The Eraser Law

Even though many teenagers seem to be aware of the perils of the disinhibition effect and oversharing online, that awareness varies.

The Right to Be Forgotten

California's Eraser law is similar to a European Union directive that allows all Europeans to object to anything on the Internet that is related to the individual making the complaint. For instance, in 2008, when Max Mosley, a Formula One racecar driver, was secretly videotaped having sadomasochistic sex with several prostitutes, he had the legal right to sue Google and potentially force it to filter the video out of its search engine.

The European Union is now considering a privacy law dubbed the Right to Be Forgotten law. The law would force all tech companies operating in the European Union to delete any content that related to a citizen, upon his or her request. Although the proposal is controversial—and might be found to be illegal—it does jibe with the European belief that, as Swiss law professor Rolf Weber explains, "dignity, honor, and the right to private life" are fundamental. The right to be forgotten is based on French law, which allows convicted criminals who have served out their sentences to protest if their criminal records are made public.

Quoted in Eugene K. Chow, "Learning from Europe's 'Right to Be Forgotten,'" *Huffington Post*, September 9, 2013. www.huffingtonpost.com.

Also, because the technology of the smartphone makes it so easy to snap a picture and post it online, lapses in good judgment happen. To help teens clean up their online identities, teachers and guidance counselors are educating students about how to find and delete inappropriate posts and pictures or change vulgar or childish screen names and e-mail addresses. Even privacy-savvy teens may not be aware that evidence of illegal activity—like underage drinking or marijuana use—can draw the attention of law enforcement officials and prevent them from getting a government security clearance later in life. Such clearances are often needed to qualify for high-paying technical jobs if the company contracts with the US government.

California has tried to address the issue by passing a law, dubbed the Eraser law, that allows teenagers to erase anything on the Internet that they later regret, such as tweets, photographs, or videos. Beginning in 2015 websites must allow California youth to delete their own content. Critics of the law point out that this means websites will be required to collect more information from users, like their age and whether or not they live in California, which erodes their privacy even further. They also note that almost every social media site allows the user to delete their own material already and that the law does nothing about content that is downloaded or reposted by others.

Sexting

The content that often causes teens the most regret is the sext—a text message that includes a nude or seminude picture of the sender. Some researchers include in their definition photographs or videos sent from a desktop or tablet computer, and some omit suggestive photos that have no nudity or nude photos that have no sexual content. The most common statistic about the prevalence of sexting is from a study by the National Campaign to Prevent Teen and Unplanned Pregnancy, which found that 20 percent of teenagers had sent nude or seminude photographs of themselves. This alarming figure has since been disputed. A 2011 article in *Pediatrics* notes that the study used an Internet panel that included eighteen- and nineteen-year-olds rather than a population sample of minors, and that their definition of *sext* included photographs that were merely suggestive and might "be no more revealing than what someone might see at a beach."[56] A study by the University of New Hampshire of 1,560 ten- to seventeen-year-olds found that only 1 percent of them had appeared in or created sexually explicit nude or seminude photographs, and about 5.9 percent had received such photographs. The Pew Research Center found that 4 percent of teens aged twelve to seventeen have sent sexts. It is likely that that percentage increases as the teens get older.

Sexting has become part of teen dating culture—sometimes referred to as the hookup culture—which is heavily influenced by digital communication. In the hookup culture, teens flirt and court each other by text or on social media sites, and it is common for boys to send X-rated pictures or propositions to girls. "Teens explained to us

Teen dating culture now often includes the practice of sexting. Teens who think they are just flirting or goofing around by texting or posting sexually suggestive photos are endangering themselves in a variety of ways.

how sexually suggestive images have become a form of relationship currency,"[57] said Amanda Lenhart, who authored the Pew sexting study. She explained that sexts were often shared between teens who were courting or already in a relationship, and they sometimes took the place of sexual activity. A boy will often pressure a girl to send him a sext as a way of letting the girl know he is interested in her. "I felt like if I didn't do it," one teen admitted, "they wouldn't continue to talk to me."[58] NBC News reports that boys who exert this kind of pressure do not mean to be hostile or demeaning; they think they are just flirting and goofing around.

Psychologist Catherine Steiner-Adair, author of *The Big Disconnect: Protecting Childhood and Family Relationships in the Digital Age*, believes that boys have learned from the media to treat girls like sexual objects and that overexposure to sexual images, pornography, and sexually graphic language has reduced their shock value for both sexes. In fact, sexts are often passed around by both boys and girls as entertainment and are usually not seen as shocking. One boy showed Steiner-Adair pornographic notes that his friends had sent his girlfriend from his Facebook account as a joke. When Steiner-Adair asked the boy why he thought the notes had turned so nasty, he said, "It didn't turn nasty. That's the norm for our generation."[59]

Susannah Stern, an associate professor at the University of San Diego, thinks sexting is so common because adolescents are steeped in media messages that show sexualized behavior as normal. She tells the *New York Times*, "They're practicing to be a part of adult culture, . . . a culture of sexualization and of putting yourself out there to validate who you are and that you matter."[60]

Sexting and Child Pornography

That does not mean that teenage girls do not feel any embarrassment when a private sext goes public. In Lacey, Washington, one girl's life was turned upside down after sending a sext to her boyfriend. Eighth grader Margarite took a naked picture of herself and sent it to Isaiah, a boy she had just started dating. After they broke up, Isaiah forwarded the picture to Margarite's ex-friend, who then, with the help of another girl, forwarded it to about seventy people. By the next day virtually the entire school had seen the picture, and Margarite was mortified. When parents complained, Margarite, Isaiah, and the two girls were pulled out of class and questioned by the police. After finding out what happened, the county prosecutor charged both Isaiah and the two girls with dissemination of child pornography, a class C felony. They spent the night in the county's juvenile detention center. "I didn't know it was against the law,"[61] Isaiah told the *New York Times*.

The prosecutor eventually downgraded the charge to telephone harassment, which would keep the case out of court and require only community service. However, by then the picture had gone viral and Margarite was being harassed not only about the picture, but about her role in the incident. People wanted to know why she was not arrested and charged also. The backlash against her might have been much less if the other teens had not been charged with child pornography, but Washington does not have an antisexting law. Because child pornography penalties are so harsh, some states have created laws that punish teenaged sexting offenders less severely, usually with community service. Seventeen states now have laws that address minors and sexting, but there is still no federal legislation.

Margarite's story is a case of sexting that turned into cyberbullying, but most incidences of sexting do not end that way. Still, it is an extreme example of what can happen when a teen acts on feelings of disinhibition in an online context. And it is a prime example of how foolish it is to believe that anything transmitted digitally will be kept private.

Chapter Five

Cyberbullying

On Labor Day weekend, 2012, fifteen-year-old Audrie Pott went to a small party in the heart of Silicon Valley, California. That summer she had been experimenting with drinking, and by 9:30 p.m. on the night of the party she was so drunk that she passed out. *Rolling Stone*, which did an in-depth story on the incident, reported that three boys who had watched Pott making out with two different people during the party carried her up to a bedroom, stripped her, penetrated her with their fingers, and drew on her naked body with Sharpies. They also took pictures of her with their smartphones.

When Pott woke up she had no memory of what happened. Terrified, she washed off as much of the marker as she could and went home. On her computer she desperately tried to find out what had happened to her. She begged the boys not to share the pictures, but soon they were circulating among her classmates. "My life is over," she wrote to a boy on Facebook. "I ruined my life and I don't even remember how."[62]

Pott went to school that week and endured escalating taunts from the other kids. The following week, one of her best friends yelled at her in the school quad, chastising her for her behavior at the party. Pott could not take it anymore. She asked her mother to pick her up from school and went directly to her bedroom. Twenty minutes later, her mother found her hanging from a belt attached to the showerhead in her bathroom. Paramedics restarted her heart, but it was too late. Two days later, she was taken off life support so her organs could be donated.

What Is Cyberbullying?

The Pew Research Center defines cyberbullying as "deliberately using digital media to communicate false, embarrassing, or hostile information about another person."[63] It can take many forms, from rumor spreading and intimidation via text message to elaborate online hoaxes. Cyberbullies commonly create websites or social media pages designed to taunt and shame their victims, such as the one a sixteen-year-old girl casually described in a Pew focus group: "There's this boy in my anatomy class who everybody hates. . . . He always wants to work in our group and I hate it. And we started this thing, some girl in my class started this I Hate [Name] MySpace thing. So everybody in school goes on it to comment bad things about this boy."[64]

Technically savvy perpetrators hack into their victims' accounts and impersonate them or gain access to their private data and share it online. Cyberbullies stalk their victims, sending them dozens—even hundreds—of threatening texts or posts a day. Denigrating photos are created with image editing tools like Photoshop and circulated. Gay or lesbian students are outed, and straight students are portrayed as gay. The proliferation of cell phones among young people has only made cyberbullying more common; perpetrators can send texts, photographs, and video quickly and easily to entire peer groups before the victim is even aware that he or she is a target.

Pew researchers state that cyberbullying "can cause profound psychosocial outcomes including depression, anxiety, severe isolation, and, tragically, suicide."[65] Researchers believe that cyberbullying is more damaging than traditional bullying because the audience is usually not restricted to the people physically present at a bullying incident; cyberbullies often humiliate their victims by making sure everyone in the victim's peer group knows about the humiliation. Anonymity is also frequently cited as a difference between cyberbullying and traditional bullying, but researchers Alice Marwick and danah boyd disagree. They believe that "while online perpetrators may appear to be anonymous, this does not mean that victims do not know the perpetrators or cannot figure out who is harassing them."[66] Marwick and boyd cite a study that found that 82 percent of the victims in their sample group knew their perpetrators and that 41 percent were friends or ex-friends.

Cyberbullying and Middle School

Research has found that cyberbullying is a common occurrence among teenagers, though Amanda Lenhart has found that most of what adults consider to be bullying is seen by teens as drama or mean-ness, and the term *cyberbullying* is reserved for the most vicious at-tacks. A 2011 survey found that 88 percent of teens have witnessed other people be mean or cruel on social networking sites, 15 percent have been the target of online meanness, and 17 percent have been bullied via text message or online.

Middle school seems to be the time when cyberbullying is most prevalent, though older children are more technologically savvy and can orchestrate more damaging attacks. At Benjamin Franklin Middle School in New Jersey, guidance counselors are overwhelmed by complaints about cyberbullying—often between ex-friends. In other middle schools—like the one Audrie Pott and her assault-ers attended—cyberbullying can be more predatory. The boys in Pott's middle school class frequently teased and harassed the girls about their bodies while pressuring them to text them topless pictures

An image of Audrie Pott (displayed during a 2013 news conference) offers a tragic reminder of where cyberbullying can lead. According to news reports, Pott killed herself after photos began circulating showing her being sexually assaulted at a party.

of themselves. One of the boys who assaulted Pott was the ringleader of the bullies in middle school. A student remembers, "He would pick on one person to make fun of for a few weeks, then move on to another."[67]

Why Cyberbullying Is So Easy

One reason cyberbullying is so common among teenagers is the online disinhibition effect. Teenagers tend to find cyberbullying more appealing than traditional bullying because they feel invisible and anonymous online. This allows them to disconnect more easily from their personal code of morality, which is still under development in adolescents. This disconnection is called deindividuation. Deindividuation—which literally means the loss of a person's sense of individuality and personal responsibility—is thought to be behind most of the atrocities that human beings have committed while disguised by masks or uniforms, such as those perpetrated by the Ku Klux Klan or soldiers in Nazi Germany. Deindividuation also causes people to copy the behavior of their peers when they are in a group. This does not have to be negative; for instance, people in an exercise class will often put in much more effort than they would if they were exercising alone. But it is also the reason that uninvolved bystanders join a lynch mob—or join in a bullying episode. Pew found that 67 percent of teens have witnessed others joining online harassment, and 21 percent admitted that they have joined in themselves. The authors of *Cyber Bullying: Bullying in the Digital Age* found that teens thought "cyberbullying was safer than traditional bullying because it was anonymous and they were less likely to get caught and it was easier because it didn't involve face-to-face confrontations."[68]

> "On Facebook, you can be as mean as you want."[69]
>
> —An eighth-grade girl.

Another characteristic of the Internet that causes the online disinhibition effect is asynchronous communication. This means that online communication is disjointed; a person writing a social media post, for instance, does not see the reaction of the intended recipient. In fact, he or she does not know when—or if—the post will be read. Teenagers who cyberbully rarely interact with their victims online in real time, such as in a chat room or an instant message. And since there is no visible victim, the harm can seem less real than it would if the bullying was face-to-face. Psychologist Graham Jones explains, "In the real world people subconsciously monitor the behavior of others around them and adapt their own behavior accordingly. . . . Online we do not have such feedback mechanisms."[69] Teenagers have confirmed that this is part of the appeal of acting out conflicts online. As one eighth-grade girl told the *New York Times*, "It's easier to fight online, because you feel more brave and in control. On Facebook, you can be as mean as you want."[70]

Cyberbullying and Sexual Assault

Though cyberbullying takes place online, it does not stay there. It is primarily just a tool of bullies who want to maximize their victims' humiliation while minimizing risk to themselves. But eventually, cyberbullying manifests back into the real world of lunchrooms and school hallways. In Audrie Pott's case, a cell phone with a camera turned a sexual assault into an opportunity to shame and humiliate a young woman in front of her entire peer group. Cyberbullying was the act of spreading the word. And the message the boys were spreading with their pictures was that Pott got what she deserved. After her death, when teachers discussed the incident in their classes, they found that most of the students blamed the victim. "In every single class, somebody raised their hand and said, 'Well, wasn't she drunk?'" says Jessica Hayes, a former classmate. "And 'I thought she was drunk.' And 'She made out with two boys.' 'She was drunk and I'm sure she liked it.'"[71]

Pott's suicide is one of a string of teen suicides that have been linked to cyberbullying. One such event involved twelve-year-old Rebecca Sedwick of Winter Haven, Florida, who jumped to her death on September 9, 2013, after being cyberbullied for a year by a group of girls. Although two of the alleged bullies were arrested, the charges against them were later dropped. Experts say that it is very difficult to prove cause and effect between bullying and suicide because the victim often has mental health issues. However, according to Yale University, teens who are bullied are two to nine

Researchers say that cyberbullying is easier than face-to-face bullying because perpetrators rarely see the reaction of their victims. Cyberbullies also feel safety in online anonymity.

times more likely to consider suicide, and a study in Britain found that at least half of all teen suicides are related to bullying.

Many of these suicides stem from a combination of sexual assault and cyberbullying. According to the Rape, Abuse and Incest National Network, a sexual assault happens in the United States every two minutes, and almost 50 percent of the victims are minors. Because of the proliferation of cell phones, many of these assaults are now photographed or videotaped. This is especially common when the assault is committed by classmates who think they are playing a prank rather than committing a rape. Laurie Halse

The Internet Troll

Trolling is the practice of leaving inflammatory, hateful, and often off-topic messages in an online community. Trolls frequent chat rooms, blogs, and the comment sections of everything from online magazine articles to YouTube videos. A troll's goal is to start trouble by making people angry or instigating an argument. Similar to a cyberbully, a troll often uses hate speech to attack an individual, though the target is usually chosen at random and is not stalked from site to site. Instead, trolls tend to stake out their territories and become associated with a particular website.

It is hard to say what motivates a troll, but people who randomly antagonize others for fun often do so because it makes them feel powerful. Trolls are commonly thought to be people with little power or status in society who start trouble on the Internet because they can do so anonymously. However, Professor Tom Postmes, who has been studying trolling behavior for years, says that anyone can take pleasure from trolling. "Like football hooligans, they have family and live at home but when they go to a match the enjoyment comes from finding a context in which you can let go, or to use the familiar phrase 'take a moral vacation.'"

Quoted in Tim Adams, "How the Internet Created an Age of Rage," *Guardian* (Manchester, UK), July 23, 2011. www.theguardian.com.

Anderson, an author of young adult novels who speaks to schools about rape, told *Rolling Stone*, "What really strikes me is that, when it comes to recording sexual assaults and wanting to show it off, the young men committing them are not seeing them as crimes, they see them as pranks. And there's no point in pulling a prank unless you share it."[72]

While these digital recordings sometimes give prosecutors the evidence they need to punish the offenders, their existence also means that the torment these girls endure never really ends. Once the pictures are shared online, they can lead to years of humiliation and bullying. And the way laws are written now, no Internet provider can be forced to take down content. According to Lori Andrews, director of the Institute for Science, Law and Technology in Chicago, "I could sue the *New York Times* for invading my privacy or *Rolling Stone* for defaming me. But I couldn't sue and get my picture off a website called sluttyseventhgraders.com."[73]

Legal Recourse for Cyberbullying

Forty-nine states have antibullying laws, and eighteen of those include provisions for cyberbullying. All require schools to have a policy in place, and they grant the schools varying powers to address the issues. But even in those states that have antibullying statutes, schools are often unsure about their authority, especially when it comes to their ability to search a student's cell phone or punish students for off-campus speech.

Judges also struggle with issues about privacy and protected speech in these cases, and rulings have been inconsistent and often come after protracted investigations. Some parents have managed to sue schools after the fact for not protecting their children from cyberbullying. But in at least one instance, a parent has successfully sued a school for disciplining a child. In Beverly Hills, California, a father sued the school district for suspending his daughter for two days after she made a defamatory video about another girl and posted it on YouTube. The video was filmed off campus, and the judge ruled that it was protected speech. "What incensed me," the girl's father told the *New York Times*, "was that these people were going to suspend my daughter for something that happened outside of school."[74] The school district was forced to pay $107,150 for the family's legal fees. That ruling has made many school districts think twice before disciplining students for activities that happen off school grounds.

> "I couldn't sue and get my picture off a website called sluttyseventh graders.com."[73]
>
> —*Lori Andrews, legal specialist.*

Who Can Help?

Because it is difficult for the law to address and prevent cyberbullying, and because schools are sometimes limited when bullying happens off school grounds, many advocacy groups are trying to tackle the problem by raising awareness among teenagers and their parents. Parents are encouraged to make an effort to understand the technologies their teenagers use and to talk openly with them on a regular basis about what goes on online. Concentrating on effective communication, studies have found, is more effective than installing online monitoring devices. The advice to keep the computer in a public space in the house instead of in a teen's bedroom—while still appearing on antibullying sites like the National Crime Prevention Council's cyberbullying web page—is already outdated, since half of all teenagers carry a smartphone.

MTV has an interactive website called A Thin Line that gives teenagers who experience cyberbullying and harassment tools and support. It encourages teens to talk with a trusted adult, document all cyberbullying, and report the behavior to Internet service pro-

Experts say that candid conversations between parents and teenagers about cell phone use and about relationships and life in general are more effective at preventing or addressing cyberbullying than are online monitoring devices.

How Is the Internet like Halloween?

In the late 1970s Edward Diener conducted an experiment on which the modern theory of deindividuation is based. On Halloween night his team turned twenty-seven homes into makeshift laboratories. As the children came to the door, a woman told them they could each have one piece of candy. She then left the bowl with the children and went back into the house. Half of the time she asked each of them to say their names and tell her where they lived. If they came to the door with an adult, they were not included in the study.

The results were dramatic. The kids who had to say their names cheated the least—less than 10 percent stole candy if they were alone, and about 20 percent stole if they were in a group. If they were anonymous, 20 percent stole when alone, and almost 60 percent stole in a group. However, if the kids were all masked—anonymous both to the woman and to each other—they all took as much candy as they could. The study demonstrated that the more anonymous a person feels in a group, the more he or she follows the will of the group.

Deindividuation should not be confused with conformity, which is about inclusion and fitting in. Deindividuation is about doing things in a group that a person would not dare to do alone.

viders. If the abuse escalates, teens should report it to their schools or law enforcement officials, or they can talk with a specialist online. MTV has also partnered with the Massachusetts Institute of Technology, which is developing a computer program that can recognize terms commonly associated with bullying. "The idea is that if someone tries to post an offensive statement, the potential bully would receive a message such as 'Are you sure you want to send this?' and some educational material about bullying may pop up,"[75] CNN reported. Henry Lieberman, who oversees the project, explained that the point was not to ban people, but to make them stop and think. "If they reflect on their behavior, and they read about the experience of others, many kids will talk themselves out of it,"[76] he said.

An Evolving Issue

The cell phone has made the age-old problem of bullying far worse for its victims. Pictures and videos can spread through entire schools in minutes and exist online indefinitely, destroying reputations and self-esteem and sometimes ending lives. Unfortunately, the law is not evolving as fast as the technology, and while some states have tried to address the problem with cyberbullying statutes, those laws are largely ineffective. At the moment, the best chance to curb cyberbullying and prevent tragedies like Audrie Pott's suicide may be for teens to regulate each other by putting social pressure on the bullies rather than on the victims, and by learning about the consequences of misusing technology. As Pott's mother, Sheila Pott, said to journalist Katie Couric on her talk show, *Katie*, "A smartphone can be a loaded weapon in the wrong hands."[77]

"A smartphone can be a loaded weapon in the wrong hands."[77]

—Sheila Pott, mother of a cyberbullying victim.

Introduction: A Teen's Most Prized Possession

1. Quoted in John Henley, "Teenagers and Technology: 'I'd Rather Give Up My Kidney than My Phone,'" *Guardian* (Manchester, UK), July 16, 2010. www.theguardian.com.

2. Quoted in Henley, "Teenagers and Technology."

Chapter One: Cell Phones and Social Development

3. Quoted in Marguerite Reardon, "Teens View Cell Phones as Essential," CNET News, September 15, 2008. http://news.cnet .com.

4. Gwenn Schurgin O'Keeffe and Kathleen Clarke-Pearson, "The Impact of Social Media on Children, Adolescents, and Families," *Pediatrics*, April 1, 2011. http://pediatrics.aappublications.org.

5. Alice Marwick, "Teens Text More than Adults, but They're Still Just Teens," Daily Beast, May 20, 2012. www.thedailybeast.com.

6. Quoted in James H. Burnett III, "How Young Is Too Young for a Phone?," *Boston Globe*, July 8, 2012. www.boston.com.

7. Quoted in Bethany L. Blair and Anne C. Fletcher, "The Only 13-Year-Old on Planet Earth Without a Cell Phone: Meanings of Cell Phones in Early Adolescents' Everyday Lives," *Journal of Adolescent Research*, March 1, 2011. http://libres.uncg.edu.

8. Quoted in Blair and Fletcher, "The Only 13-Year-Old on Planet Earth Without a Cell Phone."

9. Quoted in Elisa Batista, "She's Gotta Have It: Cell Phone," *Wired*, May 16, 2003. www.wired.com.

10. Quoted in Bianca Bosker, "What Really Happens on a Teen Girl's iPhone," *Huffington Post*, May 23, 2013. www.huffington post.com.

11. Quoted in Lilli Tilahun, "Texting Teens Increase 40 Percent in 3 Years," *ThreeSixty*, September 24, 2010. www.threesixtyjournalism.org.

12. Quoted in Tilahun, "Texting Teens Increase 40 Percent in 3 Years."

13. Quoted in Berkman Center for Internet & Society and Pew Research Center, "Highlights from Focus Groups," Youth and Media. http://youthandmedia.org.

14. Quoted in *dmlcentral* (blog), "An Analytical Take on Youth, Social Networking, and Web 2.0: A Few Moments with Amanda Lenhart," May 2012. http://dmlcentral.net.

15. Michael Osit, comment on Lisa Belkin, "Taking a Hammer to the Cell Phone," *Motherlode* (blog), *New York Times*, April 13, 2009. http://parenting.blogs.nytimes.com.

16. Donna Moss, "Texting, Texting 123 Part Three," *The Intelligent Divorce* (blog), *Psychology Today*, June 3, 2013. www.psychologytoday.com.

17. Moss, "Texting, Texting 123 Part Three."

18. Quoted in *dmlcentral* (blog), "An Analytical Take on Youth, Social Networking, and Web 2.0."

Chapter Two: Cell Phones and Addiction

19. A Day Without Media, "24 Hours: Unplugged." http://withoutmedia.wordpress.com.

20. Quoted in A Day Without Media, "24 Hours."

21. Quoted in Mez Breeze, "A Quiet Killer: Why Video Games Are So Addictive," Next Web, January 12, 2013. http://thenextweb.com.

22. Bill Davidow, "Exploiting the Neuroscience of Internet Addiction," *Atlantic*, July 18, 2012. www.theatlantic.com.

23. Suzanne Phillips, "Teens Sleeping with Cell Phones: A Clear and Present Danger," PBS.org. www.pbs.org.

24. Diana I. Tamir and Jason P. Mitchell, "Disclosing Information About the Self Is Intrinsically Rewarding," *PNAS*, May 22, 2012. http://wjh.harvard.edu.

25. Quoted in Alan Mozes, "Can Excessive Cellphone Use Become an Addiction?," *U.S. News & World Report*, December 4, 2012. http://health.usnews.com.

26. Quoted in Phillips, "Teens Sleeping with Cell Phones."

27. Moss, "Texting, Texting 123 Part Three."

28. Quoted in Tony Dokoupil, "Is the Web Driving Us Mad?," *Newsweek*, July 9, 2012. http://mag.newsweek.com.

29. Quoted in Dokoupil, "Is the Web Driving Us Mad?"

30. Nicholas Carr, *The Shallows: What the Internet Is Doing to Our Brains*. London: Atlantic, 2011, p. 12.

31. Carr, *The Shallows*, p. 30.

32. Carr, *The Shallows*, p. 215.

Chapter Three: Texting While Driving

33. Quoted in Joe Angio, "Driver's Ed," AT&T Insider. http://insider.att.com.

34. Quoted in Irene Lacher, "Werner Herzog's Cautionary Tale for Texters," *Los Angeles Times*, August 16, 2013. www.latimes.com.

35. Quoted in CBS New York, "Study: Texting and Driving Kills More Teens Annually than Drinking and Driving," May 9, 2013. http://newyork.cbslocal.com.

36. Quoted in Michelle Healy, "Study: Teens Who Text and Drive Take Even More Risks," *USA Today*, May 13, 2013. www.usatoday.com.

37. Quoted in Jim Vertuno, "Cell Phones Raise Teen Driving Deaths," NBC News, May 6, 2010. www.nbcnews.com.

38. Quoted in Genevra Pittman, "ADHD, Texting a Dangerous Combination," *Chicago Tribune*, August 13, 2013. http://my.chicagotribune.com.

39. Quoted in Healy, "Study."

40. Emily O'Malley Olsen, Ruth A. Shults, and Danice K. Eaton, "Texting While Driving and Other Risky Motor Vehicle Behaviors Among US High School Students," *Pediatrics*, May 13, 2013. http://pediatrics.aappublications.org.

41. Randye Hoder, "'Yo, I'm Driving. I'll Text You When It's Safe,'" *Motherlode* (blog), *New York Times*, September 25, 2013. http://parenting.blogs.nytimes.com.

42. Hoder, "'Yo, I'm Driving. I'll Text You When It's Safe.'"

43. Quoted in Larry Copeland, "Texting in Traffic: Adults Worse than Teens," *USA Today*, March 28, 2013. www.usatoday.com.

44. Quoted in KJ Dell'Antonia, "Teenagers Say Parents Text and Drive," *Motherlode* (blog), *New York Times*, September 27, 2012. http://parenting.blogs.nytimes.com.

45. Anne T. McCartt, Charles M. Farmer, and James W. Jenness, "Perceptions and Experiences of Participants in a Study of In-Vehicle Monitoring of Teenage Drivers," *Traffic Injury Prevention*, 2010. www.tandfonline.com.

Chapter Four: Oversharing and Sexting

46. Quoted in Jeremy Dean, "Six Causes of Online Disinhibition," *PsyBlog*, August 19, 2010. www.spring.org.uk.

47. Dean, "Six Causes of Online Disinhibition."

48. Cecilia Kang, "Parting with Privacy with a Quick Click," *Washington Post*, May 8, 2011. www.washingtonpost.com.

49. Trend Micro, "The Dangers of Posting Credit Cards, IDs on Instagram and Twitter," Virus/Malware/Hacking/Security News, April 12, 2012. www.viruss.eu.

50. Quoted in Protect My Rep, "Mistakes We Make," http://protectmyrep.org.

51. Quoted in Protect My Rep, "Who Is Watching?," http://protectmyrep.org.

52. Quoted in Natasha Singer, "They Loved Your G.P.A. Then They Saw Your Tweets," *New York Times*, November 9, 1913. www.nytimes.com.

53. Will Oremus, "Of Course Colleges Are Reading Kid's Tweets and Facebook Posts," *Slate*, November 11, 2013. www.slate.com.

54. Quoted in *dmlcentral* (blog), "An Analytical Take on Youth, Social Networking, and Web 2.0."

55. Jacqui Cheng, "What Inner City Kids Know About Social Media, and Why We Should Listen," Medium. https://medium.com.

56. Kimberly J. Mitchell, David Finkelhor, Lisa M. Jones, and Janis Wolak, "Prevalence and Characteristics of Youth Sexting: A National Study," *Pediatrics*, December 5, 2011. http://pediatrics.aappublications.org.

57. Amanda Lenhart, "Teens and Sexting," Pew Internet & American Life Project, December 15, 2009. www.pewinternet.org.

58. Quoted in Lenhart, "Teens and Sexting."

59. Quoted in Abigail Pesta, "Boys Also Harmed by Teen 'Hookup' Culture, Experts Say," NBC News, August 15, 2013. www.nbcnews.com.

60. Quoted in Jan Hoffman, "A Girl's Nude Photo, and Altered Lives," *New York Times*, March 26, 2011. www.nytimes.com.

61. Quoted in Hoffman, "A Girl's Nude Photo, and Altered Lives."

Chapter Five: Cyberbullying

62. Quoted in Nina Burleigh, "Sexting, Shame and Suicide," *Rolling Stone*, September 17, 2013. www.rollingstone.com.

63. Quoted in O'Keeffe and Clarke-Pearson, "The Impact of Social Media on Children, Adolescents, and Families."

64. Quoted in Amanda Lenhart, "Data Memo: Major Findings," Pew Internet & American Life Project, June 27, 2007. http://pewinternet.org.

65. Quoted in O'Keeffe and Clarke-Pearson, "The Impact of Social Media on Children, Adolescents, and Families."

66. danah boyd and Alice Marwick, "The Conundrum of Visibility: Youth Safety and the Internet," *Journal of Children and Media*, 2009. www.danah.org.

67. Quoted in Burleigh, "Sexting, Shame and Suicide."

68. Robin M. Kowalski, Susan P. Limber, and Patricia W. Agatston, *Cyber Bullying: Bullying in the Digital Age*. Malden, MA: Blackwell, 2008, p. 59.

69. Quoted in Alan Martin, "Online Disinhibition and the Psychology of Trolling," *Wired UK*, May 30, 2013. www.wired.co.uk.

70. Quoted in Jan Hoffman, "Online Bullies Pull Schools into the Fray," *New York Times*, June 27, 2010. www.nytimes.com.

71. Quoted in Burleigh, "Sexting, Shame and Suicide."

72. Quoted in Burleigh, "Sexting, Shame and Suicide."

73. Quoted in Burleigh, "Sexting, Shame and Suicide."

74. Quoted in Hoffman, "Online Bullies Pull Schools into the Fray."

75. Quoted in Elizabeth Landau, "When Bullying Goes High-Tech," CNN, April 15, 2013. http://edition.cnn.com.

76. Quoted in Landau, "When Bullying Goes High-Tech."

77. Quoted in Katie Couric, "Cyber-Bullied to Death: A Mom's Heartbreaking Discovery," October 14, 2013. http://katiecouric .com.

Related Organizations and Websites

Centers for Disease Control and Prevention (CDC)

4770 Buford Hwy. NE, MS F-63
Atlanta, GA 30341-3717
phone: (800) 232-4636
website: www.cdc.gov

On its distracted driving page, the CDC provides information, resources, statistics, and studies related to distracted driving.

Cyberbullying Research Center

website: www.cyberbullying.us

The Cyberbullying Research Center is dedicated to providing up-to-date information about the nature, extent, causes, and consequences of cyberbullying among adolescents.

Distraction.gov

website: www.distraction.gov

The official US government website for distracted driving. Distraction.gov provides facts, resources, and legal information about distracted driving.

Family Online Safety Institute (FOSI)

400 Seventh St. NW, Suite 306
Washington, DC 20004
website: www.fosi.org

An international nonprofit organization, FOSI works to make the online world safer for kids and their families. FOSI convenes leaders in industry, government, and the nonprofit sectors to collaborate and innovate new solutions and policies in the field of online safety. FOSI promotes Internet safety through research, resources, events, and special projects.

It Can Wait
website: www.itcanwait.com

An initiative by major US cell phone carriers that focuses on educating people—especially teens—about the dangers of texting and driving. The website contains educational videos, resources, and statistics.

Pew Research Center
1615 L St. NW, Suite 700
Washington, DC 20036
phone: (202) 419-4300 • fax: (202) 419-4349
e-mail: info@pewresearch.org
website: www.pewresearch.org

The Pew Research Center is a nonpartisan, nonprofit social research organization that provides information on the issues, attitudes, and trends shaping America and the world. Its Pew Internet & American Life Project produces reports exploring the impact of the Internet on families, communities, work, home, daily life, education, health care, and civic and political life.

StopBullying.gov
website: www.stopbullying.gov

StopBullying.gov is a federal government website that provides information from various government agencies on what bullying is, what cyberbullying is, who is at risk, and how people can prevent and respond to bullying.

A Thin Line
website: www.athinline.org

MTV's A Thin Line campaign was developed to empower teenagers to identify, respond to, and stop the spread of digital abuse. It provides information, resources, and support.

Unslut Project

website: www.unslutproject.com

The Unslut Project promotes gender equality, sex positivity, and comprehensive, age-appropriate sex education for all ages. This is a collaborative space for sharing stories and creating awareness about sexual bullying, cyberbullying, shaming, and related issues.

We Stop Hate

website: www.westophate.org

We Stop Hate is a nonprofit program dedicated to raising self-esteem in teens (teen esteem) through various social media platforms that engage teens to help each other gain confidence.

Wired Safety

website: www.wiredsafety.org

Wired Safety is the largest and oldest online safety, education, and help group in the world. It provides one-to-one help, extensive information, and education to cyberspace users of all ages on a myriad of Internet and interactive technology safety, privacy, and security issues.

For Further Research

Books

Mark Bauerlein, *The Digital Divide: Arguments for and Against Facebook, Google, Texting, and the Age of Social Networking*. New York: Tarcher, 2011.

Nicholas Carr, *The Shallows: What the Internet Is Doing to Our Brains*. New York: Norton, 2011.

Ted Claypoole and Theresa M. Payton, *Protecting Your Internet Identity: Are You Naked Online?* Lanham, MD: Rowman & Littlefield, 2012.

Matt Ivester, *lol . . . OMG! What Every Student Needs to Know About Online Reputation Management, Digital Citizenship and Cyberbullying*. Reno, NV: Serra Knight, 2011.

Gregory L. Jantz, *Hooked: The Pitfalls of Media, Technology and Social Networking*. Lake Mary, FL: Siloam, 2012.

Larry D. Rosen, *iDisorder: Understanding Our Obsession with Technology and Overcoming Its Hold on Us*. New York: Palgrave Macmillan, 2012.

Catherine Steiner-Adair and Teresa H. Barker, *The Big Disconnect: Protecting Childhood and Family Relationships in the Digital Age*. New York: HarperCollins, 2013.

Internet Sources

Bianca Bosker, "What Really Happens on a Teen Girl's iPhone," *Huffington Post*, May 23, 2013. http://www.huffingtonpost.com/2013/05/23/teen-iphone_n_3322095.html.

Bill Davidow, "Exploiting the Neuroscience of Internet Addiction," *Atlantic*, July 18, 2012. http://www.theatlantic.com/health

/archive/2012/07/exploiting-the-neuroscience-of-internet
-addiction/259820/.

Jeremy Dean, "Six Causes of Online Disinhibition," *PsyBlog*, August 19, 2010. http://www.spring.org.uk/2010/08/six-causes-of-on
line-disinhibition.php.

Tony Dokoupil, "Is the Internet Making Us Crazy?," *Newsweek*,
July 9, 2012. http://mag.newsweek.com/2012/07/08/is-the-internet
-making-us-crazy-what-the-new-research-says.html.

Amanda Lenhart et al., *Teens and Mobile Phones*, Pew Internet &
American Life Project, Pew Research Center, April 20, 2010. http://
pewinternet.org/Reports/2010/Teens-and-Mobile-Phones/Sum
mary-of-findings.aspx.

Amanda Lenhart et al., *Teens, Kindness and Cruelty on Social Network
Sites*, Pew Internet & American Life Project, Pew Research Cen-
ter, November 9, 2011. www.fosi.org/images/stories/research/PIP
-Teens-Kindness-Cruelty-SNS-Report-Nov-2011.pdf.

Mary Madden et al., *Teens and Technology 2013*, Pew Internet &
American Life Project, Pew Research Center, March 13, 2013. www
.pewinternet.org/Reports/2013/Teens-and-Tech.aspx.

Alice Marwick, "Teens Text More than Adults, but They're Still Just
Teens," *Newsweek*, May 20, 2012. www.thedailybeast.com/news
week/2012/05/20/teens-text-more-than-adults-but-they-re-still
-just-teens.html.

Dave Mosher, "High Wired: Does Addictive Internet Use Restruc-
ture the Brain?," *Scientific American*, June 17, 2011. www.scientific
american.com/article.cfm?id=does-addictive-internet-use-restruc
ture-brain.

Peter Weber, "Could a Social Media Eraser Law Save an Oversharing Generation?," *Week*, September 20, 2013. http://theweek
.com/article/index/249988/could-a-social-media-eraser-law-save
-an-over-sharing-generation.

Index

Picture Credits

Cover: Thinkstock Images

Gary Reyes/MCT/Newscom: 54

© David Shopper/Corbis: 7

Greg Sorber/Zuma Press/Newscom: 37

Thinkstock Images: 11, 15, 22, 27, 33, 43, 49, 57, 60

About the Author

Christine Wilcox writes fiction and nonfiction for young adults and adults. She has worked as an editor, an instructional designer, and a writing instructor. She lives in Richmond, Virginia, with her husband, David, and her son, Doug.